Advance
How To Get You

G000039089

"If you have a book you want to get into K-12 schools and sell in the thousands, you MUST read this book. With a friendly voice and an easy-to-read style, Hendrickson shares his journey with his own books as he steps you through the entire process from getting the book on the recommended reading list to the campaign and how to manage the publishing flow when requests land on your desk. Highly Recommended!"

— Maggie Lynch, bestselling author
of DIY Publishing books

"*How To Get Your Book Into Schools* is such a useful book! The flow reads quickly and the language is easy to understand. The unique insights Hendrickson provides into the entire process of selling a book into a school system are invaluable. Not only does he discuss the strategy involved but he explains the business side of the numbers in a way writers can understand."

— Tonya D. Price, author
Business Books For Writers

"I learned a ton about how to manage cash flow and what I need to do to get my books into schools. This book is terrific not just for high school-based writers, but for colleges, too! Read it and learn what might make sense for your author career."

— Johanna Rothman,
author and consultant

"The value of this book is a mindset change. Authors need to look at schools as a market for bulk sales, and market their books that way, instead of focusing on the individual teacher. While the teacher is a great market, if you stop there, you're neglecting a large potential market."

—Darcy Pattison, author,
MimsHouse.com
IndieKidsBooks.com

"Clear and concise! Tons of great information here that will prove to be invaluable for writers trying to bring their books to schools."

—Rigel Ailur, author,
Tales of Mimion

Also by David H. Hendrickson

Bubba Goes for Broke

Cracking the Ice

Offside

Offensive Foul

Writing as D. H. Hendrickson

Body Check

No Defense

HOW TO
GET YOUR BOOK
INTO
SCHOOLS

and
DOUBLE YOUR INCOME
with VOLUME SALES

DAVID H. HENDRICKSON

Pentucket Publishing
www.pentucketpublishing.com

How to Get Your Book Into Schools
and Double Your Income With Volume Sales

Disclaimer: All prices shown are based on those in effect in the United States at the beginning of December 2017. They are subject to change.

ISBN-13: 978-1-948134-06-4
ISBN-10: 1-948134-06-3

Table of Contents

Part III: Results!

To Brenda,
the Best Wife Ever,
who gets me through the valleys
and makes the peaks all worthwhile

HOW TO
GET YOUR BOOK
INTO
SCHOOLS

and
DOUBLE YOUR INCOME
with VOLUME SALES

INTRODUCTION

The thunderous applause from the assembled high school students washed over me. Off to my left, as I stood at the lectern waiting to speak, a boisterous group of boys began chanting the name of my novel: "*Offside! Offside! Offside!*" The applause began to fade, then built back up to a roar. In all, it lasted for almost a full minute.

It felt like a lifetime.

The students of Lynn English High School had read my novel as their assigned summer reading. And they'd loved it!

I would have been happy with any reception short of rotten tomatoes, but this took my breath away. Thoughts of all the struggles and frustrations—decades of form-letter rejections, the all-too-believable possibility that I just…did…not…have…any…talent—made this moment all the sweeter.

After my two talks, one for the freshmen and sophomores and another for the juniors and seniors, because the auditorium could not accommodate the entire student body of over sixteen hundred, I signed hundreds and hundreds of copies of the book. And for those who had forgotten their copy, I signed Post-it Notes to put inside as a substitute. I signed agenda books, backpacks, and with a Sharpie, over a dozen—I kid you not—outstretched bare arms.

Over a dozen students wanted my signature…on their arms!

I felt like a rock star.

I will always be grateful to those students of Lynn English High School for how wonderfully they treated me that day. From the girls in the front row who whispered to me before the event began, "Mr. Hendrickson, I loved your book!"…to those boys who chanted its title…to all those proffered arms, backpacks, and books for me to sign.

Other than family events, it was the greatest day of my life. A day I would wish for every writer.

This book can't promise you a day like the one I experienced. In fact, if you're as introverted as many of my writer friends are, the very thought of such a day—speaking to more than sixteen hundred students and their teachers!—might send your heart into palpitations. If so, no one is going to drag you to any podium. You can just "settle" for having all those students read your book.

Whatever the case, this book makes no absolute promises. Every situation and opportunity is unique to some degree. There may be some element of luck to your pursuit of getting your book into the hands of students. That said, a major component of luck is putting yourself into the best possible position for success. This book will try to do that for you.

It will refer to novels, because they are the most typical candidate for adoption, but there's no reason you can't apply it to your nonfiction book or other project. In fact, you can use much of the advice here to get your nonfiction book into corporations. (Don't be surprised if I release a follow-up title targeted on that specific goal.)

That said, the focus here will be on getting your book into high schools, because that is where my own experience lies, and where I believe the most fertile opportunity exists. Once again, however, there's no reason you can't use the suggestions found here to pursue students in colleges and universities, junior high schools, and even middle grades. In fact, one of the resources I describe is available for elementary schools. I'll use examples that are specific to the United States, but the ideas apply pretty much everywhere.

I'll also refer to students reading your book in the summer, because that's the typical high school assignment. However, that doesn't have to be the case. In fact, as I write this, two of my books are under consideration for adoption at a year-round school. If that happens, the book selected will become part of the basic curriculum. More often than not, though, summer reading is your optimal target and that's what I'll focus on here.

Finally, I've approached this book as a "hybrid" writer, one who pursues traditional publishing for some projects and indie publishing with others. For my short fiction, I remain in the traditional camp, where I've appeared in *Ellery Queen's Mystery Magazine* and numerous anthologies. In recent years, however, I've switched to indie publishing for my novels (for reasons that would fill a book or two all by themselves).

I do speak a bit more directly to those of you who have indie published your novel. (I'll default to trade paperbacks at CreateSpace in my examples, but will bring in IngramSpark and Lightning Source where appropriate, and I'll also discuss hardcovers.) As an indie writer, you'll have more flexibility to implement some of my suggestions, but you'll also have more work to do. I'll lay out those tasks.

If, on the other hand, you're a traditionally published writer, you can still make full use of this book. Some chapters won't apply to you, and you won't have as much direct control as an indie writer, but you can still use the techniques I describe in the upcoming chapters.

Whatever your background, I hope you all soon find your books in the hands of eager students.

PART I: THE BASICS

CHAPTER 1

What Are the Benefits?

Before we go any further, let's look at the benefits of getting your book (or books!) into schools. Some benefits are obvious, but you might overlook others. Looking at all the benefits will help you decide how much time and energy, if any, you're willing to invest.

First, it can be a *very* nice payday. Somehow, I doubt this particular benefit is catching you by surprise—*What, I could make money?*—but the magnitude might. The exact amount depends on a number of factors, most notably the size of the school, the price of your book, and the discount you offer. We'll cover those topics and more further down the line. But we're talking about thousands of dollars, and potentially more than ten thousand dollars.

Got your attention?

Just in case you buy into the allure of being a "starving artist" and feel you'll be prostituting your art if you attempt something as disgusting as a marketing campaign (*eeew, gross!*) to get your book into schools, then let me argue that point, and if I still don't convince you, then plug your nose when you cash the check and focus on the other benefits.

First, the argument. Poverty is not a virtue. Maybe those dollars are the difference between you writing full-time and not. That's a big deal and as honorable a goal as it gets. Or maybe those dollars pay for medicine for your kids. Arguably an even bigger deal.

Whatever the case, writers deserve to be paid for their expertise just like other highly trained professionals. A software engineer doesn't apologize for getting paid. Neither should you. Besides, if you do things right, you can offer attractive discounts to schools so it's a win-win situation.

Onward, then, to the second benefit.

You want readers, don't you? One of the reasons we write is to communicate. It's why we don't just stuff those pages, never to be seen, into a file cabinet, old-fashioned or electronic. So attracting readers whom you wouldn't otherwise attract is a great thing all by itself. And if they like what they read, they just might buy something else you've written. Young readers are often voracious readers. They're also at an age where they might just be devouring your work for the next fifty or more years.

Wouldn't that just be terrible?

Third, getting your book into the schools can be gratifying food for your writer's soul, sustenance for the inevitable disappointments and frustrations. If you're at all like me, you've been knocked down a lot. I'd rather not admit how many years passed before I could convince anyone to buy my stories. And then when I finally broke through, at least a little, my first novel, *Cracking the Ice*, got out the doors just as its publishing house was slamming those doors shut, locking them, and throwing away the key. That book, so dear to my heart, wasn't just published dead. Its corpse was frozen solid.

Hey, maybe everything in your writing life has been all sunshine and roses. If so, you don't need the emotional boost the rest of us do. But for us folks, having our books in the hands of students provides healing for old wounds and an armor to protect against new ones.

Fourth—and I've already mentioned this in the introduction, so I'll make this quick—you might get the opportunity to speak to the young people who read your work. That can be a wonderful experience, and if you're of sufficiently high profile, there might be an honorarium involved.

The fifth and final reward to getting your books into schools is, in some ways, the best of all. You can affect the lives of young people. Whether your readers are from affluent communities or the poorest of households, they're at a formative, often fragile, point in their lives.

You can make a difference. And that is awesome.

CHAPTER 2

How Can You Succeed?

There are multiple ways in which your book can get adopted by a school, all of them great, all of them with the benefits mentioned in the previous chapter, though to differing degrees.

The most basic distinction is whether a school buys copies of your book for all its students or instead simply puts it on a list of approved books, from which students make their own choices and their own purchases. The former is certainly the most attractive option, for multiple reasons, but don't dismiss the impact of the latter. Let's look at that possibility first.

Getting on a Recommended Reading List

If your book is on a list with a dozen or more other titles from which students purchase their own copies, then all things considered equal, you're going to get less than ten percent of those potential readers. Instead of a one-time, wonderful, fire-hose blast of sales, you'll experience something more like a steady stream over the course of a summer. Or perhaps only a trickle. Or, gasp, just a drop or two.

You might not even know that a school has put your book on its list. One would hope that those teachers who were brilliant and perceptive enough to select your title would also be considerate enough to let you know, but we all know teachers are overworked and underpaid, and it could slip through the cracks unless you somehow incentivize them to let you know.

All that said, there are advantages. First off, you made the list! Congratulations! Out of all the millions of books out there, a school chose yours. That's an outstanding achievement!

Keep in mind that there are titles that make sense for an approved list, but not for the entire school population. Some books appeal almost exclusively to one gender. Conventional wisdom in the Young Adult publishing industry has been that girls are more flexible, more willing to read books with primarily male characters involved in stereotypically male pursuits, than picky boy readers are to similarly cross over. The editor of my first novel, *Cracking the Ice*, commented that it was perfect for teenage boys and "the girls will come along."

So maybe your book appeals only to girls, or only to some sliver of the school population—lovers of mountain climbing, chess, or baroque music—and therefore isn't ideal for everyone. Or perhaps it's not ideal, really, for any of the students, but some singular characteristic about you—more on this later—has made it worthy of inclusion on the list, but not for a mandatory choice for the entire school.

Good for you! Inclusion on an approved list is infinitely better than nothing.

And there are two advantages. First off, you don't have to take any of the financial risks involved in selling large numbers of copies to a school, then waiting (and waiting) for payment. (Much more on this later.) If you're already living from payday to payday, this is a *huge* advantage.

The other positive is that as students, or more likely their parents, buy your books either online or from brick-and-mortar bookstores, those sales will factor into sales algorithms. There might be a "halo" effect to these sales. That is, you could see those sales trigger others as your book receives a more prominent placement either online or in stores.

All the Students Read Your Book

Okay, let's return now to the case where a school adopts your wonderful book for all of its students to read. There are two variations on that theme: either you sell directly to the school or the school buys from a distributor or bookstore.

Selling direct has all the obvious advantages: you get much more of the richly deserved profit, you can offer a better discount for the school, and there's no one else to foul up your deal.

I'm guessing I had you at "you get much more of the richly deserved profit."

Chapter 13 will discuss the financial details of selling your books direct. It's what I recommend for most writers. But let's talk first about going through a distributor or bookstore.

The same two advantages I listed before to students buying your books off an approved list potentially apply here, magnified a hundred-fold (or whatever the size of the school). You get much less financial reward (somewhere between 28 and

40 cents on the dollar, depending on several factors), but you take none of the risk. The school buys from the distributor or bookstore, not from you, albeit at a higher price.

Additionally, while sales algorithms and their effect on product placement are closely guarded secrets, it appears that sales through a bookstore count as sales (well, duh!), whereas sales to yourself on CreateSpace (or IngramSpark or the other alternatives) do not, even if the books are drop-shipped to a school. Don't expect an algorithm-fueled halo effect with direct sales or those through a distributor like Ingram. There might be one if you go through a bookstore.

There are prerequisites, however, to using a distributor or a bookstore as an intermediary. You'll either need to specify the "Extended Distribution" option in the CreateSpace Distribution Channels menu or, even better, use IngramSpark for distribution. This is one case where IngramSpark gives you a better royalty on those sales. We'll get into those details in Chapter 13, but for now realize that you need some distributor that either the school or bookstore will buy from.

Many schools will have an Ingram account, removing any need to get a bookstore involved. The school will buy from Ingram and you'll get an IngramSpark royalty check in due course. Or, if you've instead chosen CreateSpace Extended Distribution, the school will buy on its account with either Ingram or Baker & Taylor, and you'll get a somewhat smaller royalty check from CreateSpace.

If the school has no distributor account, however, you'll need to find a bookstore to work with. That may be easier said than done. And the financial numbers will get squeezed. The bookstore has the required distributor account, but will be an extra middleman requiring compensation. By the time you, the distributor, and the bookstore all take their cuts, there may not be much room left for a discount to the school. That may reduce your chances of a deal significantly. Additionally, you may not find a bookstore willing and able to shoulder the cash-flow issues.

So don't count on a bookstore riding in to your rescue. And if one does, keep in mind that your priority may not be its priority. When you're working direct with a school, it is your number-one priority. For a bookstore, your sale to that school may be somewhere down the line.

There's much more on this topic to come. In general, I recommend selling your book direct to the schools, but recognize that you might not be able, or willing, to take on the risks involved. If so, that's fine. Either way, we'll look at all the details so you can make an informed decision.

CHAPTER 3

How Do You Get Your Book Into Decision Makers' Hands?

For novels, the critical decision makers will almost always be teachers in, or the chair of, the English, Language, Arts (ELA) department. (At some schools, simply the English department.) These teachers won't just decide for their own classes; they'll help decide for the entire school. They won't be the final decision makers, but the process typically starts with them and will almost certainly end with them if they aren't impressed. Their opinion carries great weight going forward to the school's principal and then to the budgeting authority.

So how do you get your book into the hands of these key decision makers?

For the most part, it comes down to two basic choices: word of mouth vs. a proactive marketing campaign. Although my use of the term "proactive" might make it seem like I'm dismissing word of mouth as being too passive, that isn't the case at all. Both approaches have their advantages.

Word of Mouth

My success in getting *Offside* adopted by Lynn English High School for its entire student body came purely through word of mouth. A mother of a student there heard about the novel, and bought a copy for her son, a student at the school. He loved it enough to bring to his English teacher with the recommendation that the entire class should read it. From there, it went to the ELA chair, who then enthusiastically brought it to the school principal. Numerous hurdles remained to be cleared, which I'll talk about in due course, but the stark reality is this: *a lot* of people had to love that book, and love it *a lot,* for it to even get to the principal's desk for consideration.

That leads to the first ironclad rule in this process. Nothing else matters if you ignore this.

You must write the best possible book you can.

Shortly, I'll mention why some books might be worth investing more time, effort, and yes, money to market them because they stand a higher chance of success. But if you cynically attempt to target such opportunities and don't write the best book you can from deep inside your heart, then you're lost.

Do you really think all the people who need to go to bat for you will do so for anything but your best?

I'm not saying that I'm God's gift to writing. Far from it. I still have so much to learn, it's humbling. (It's also exciting that there's *always* something new to learn, but that's a topic unto itself.) All I'm saying is that I pour everything I have into my fiction. It's less than what the masters have to give, but I give it all I've got. And so should you. Otherwise, why bother?

Okay, sermon over.

Here's the advantage to word of mouth: it requires no marketing effort at all. No expense in terms of cost, time, or energy. Just sit back and wait until someone else goes to bat for your book. (Well, don't just sit back, of course. Write your next book with all that's deep inside you...and then the one after that...and then the one after that.) Put your time and energy into writing. There's a lot to be said for that.

The disadvantage to word of mouth is pretty obvious: you need to get lucky. Others have to do the heavy lifting for you until you show up at the end to carry it over the finish line.

I got lucky. Very lucky. In the end, I had to know what I was doing (and learn the rest) to get the deal done, but I needed a mother and her son to get everything started.

A Marketing Campaign

If you're not willing to wait for lightning to strike for you—and you can count me in that camp since I'm not waiting for a second lightning strike—then the alternative can make sense, at least for some books. Don't wait for word of mouth. Take the initiative with a marketing campaign and get your book into the hands of those first-level decision-makers.

What type of marketing campaign? In other endeavors, there are any number of possibilities. For writers, there are technically two, but in my opinion, only one that makes sense.

You could buy advertisements in publications geared for teachers. Advertisements, however, can be expensive, and even the advertising industry isn't sure why some ads trigger sales and others don't. It's a subconscious attraction to the red sports car or desire for a cold beverage or a pepperoni pizza. You need more than a subconscious noticing of your book. You need more than name recognition that pays off at some later date. You need a teacher to send an email or fill out a form asking for an examination copy. Advertisements won't be a cost-effective way of achieving that.

Instead, I advocate a direct mail campaign from you to teachers. A lot of them will throw your flier in the trash. That's the nature of the beast. But you'll have invested little—*perhaps less than a dollar per school*—and if you've done it right, enough will respond because your book has caught their attention.

That leads us to our next topic. When is a book *worth* that extra effort and expense?

CHAPTER 4

When is the Extra Effort and Expense Worth It?

Scott William Carter, a terrific writer and friend, suggests that writers apply the WIBBOW test when considering *all* of those countless things into which we can invest our time and effort.

Would I Be Better Off Writing?

WIBBOW.

It's a brilliantly simple test to make sure your fiction writing time doesn't lose out to every last promotional or marketing tool out there: your website, your mailing list, Facebook, Twitter, Instagram, YouTube, podcasts, blogging, and so on ad infinitum.

Apply the WIBBOW test to decide if you should just stick with word of mouth while you write more, or if it does in fact make sense to invest time and effort (and some money) into trying to get your book into schools. Not all books are created equal in terms of their opportunity to succeed in this area. And some books may have a specialized appeal that makes them attractive for only a few schools, requiring a minimum investment on your part.

Let's start with genre. Erotica in all its forms, including "active romance," clearly goes far beyond the boundary of what schools would deem acceptable. The same holds true for any genre loaded with gratuitous violence. At the other end of the spectrum, your faith-based novel might be so squeaky clean you'd give it both to Grandma and your pastor, but it won't work in a public school expected to maintain a separation between church and state. (A religious private school, however, could be another story.) Mystery and suspense novels that involve almost exclusively adult characters? Not as impossible, but not very likely.

The sweet spot for high schools is Young Adult fiction, for all the obvious reasons. The hero or heroine, and most of the characters, are teenagers that students can relate to. Perhaps even more to the point, those characters are dealing with typically teenage problems. When Lynn English High School selected *Offside*, the teachers were attracted, among other things, to the themes of bullying, racial problems, family dysfunction, and friendships. They also praised *Offside* for being a fast-paced book that included a lot of sports to keep their less dedicated readers interested.

Many YA titles, however, will send principals running for cover. Edgy novels involving drug use, sex, and violence may attract teenage readers and contain powerful messages they need to hear, but still be rejected if they offend too many parents' sensibilities. Principals face headaches every day and will be understandably hesitant to add more in the form of parental complaints.

That isn't to say you should pull your punches when you write your novel. To do so withers the creative spirit. Always write the your best possible book. Pull enough punches and you're left with a work that has no punch.

Just realize when it comes time to present an edgy book to schools, some of what makes it distinctive and potentially important might also work against its acceptance. Write that book, but be realistic about its chances for adoption.

So if your book isn't close to most high schools' sweet spot of acceptance, do you just give up? Not necessarily. There are special cases when you should consider a limited attempt on your part even if your book might not otherwise be considered an ideal fit.

If it's set in Lincoln City, Oregon, a small amount of effort checking with schools in that city and the surrounding areas makes sense. If you're an alum of Boston Latin High School, check with that school. Students will identify with "one of their own." Same thing with the schools in the community you live in. You're one of them; you're special. A couple of these factors have worked to my advantage. Perhaps the same will hold true for you.

PART II: PLANNING

Plan a Little for Failure,
Plan a Lot for Success

CHAPTER 5

The Foundation

It's almost instinctive in life to plan in case of failure—*How will I recover from this disaster?*—and assume that success will take care of itself. After all, doesn't success mean...you succeeded? In this endeavor, however, the opposite is true.

Your plan in the event of failure is pretty basic: assume that your modest investment in postage and materials—whether it's less than fifty dollars or more than several hundred—is not going to pay off. Assume the worst. You're going to lose it all.

If this is money you can't afford to risk, you shouldn't try this. Why? First off, because you're going to have to beat the odds to get your book adopted by a school. I'll try to help you improve your chances, but it's still at least somewhat more likely you'll strike out than it is you'll hit a home run. Secondly, and far more importantly, if you can't afford to risk a hundred dollars or maybe two in your marketing campaign, then issues like cash flow will destroy you if you succeed.

So your plan for dealing with failure is straightforward. Assume you will lose your money. If you do, keep writing more books, figure out what you might have done wrong, and decide what to change if you make another go of it.

Planning for success is a lot more complicated, but it is vital. First off, you need to have the publishing foundation in place to support selling books to schools. Let's look at what that includes. Much of this may seem obvious to you and you've already done it, but it may not be to others.

Specifically, you need to be a publisher, one that has all the look and feel of a professional publisher.

Set Up a Publishing Company

As an indie author, you've probably set up some publishing entity. If you haven't done so yet, you need to do so now. And if you previously set it up wrong, now's the best time to fix it.

Your publishing entity should sound like a press, not like an individual. For example, my entity isn't called David Hendrickson, it's called Pentucket Publishing. Yes, I know that Simon & Schuster was formed by Richard Simon and Max Schuster, but that was 1924. Things have changed just a bit since then. You really do want to sound like a publisher, not an individual.

For the purposes of this book, let's assume you call your publishing entity Big Oink Press. I'm sure you can come up with a better name than that—it would be hard to do worse—but I wanted to avoid a name already in use. (To be honest, Big Oink is also the first thing that came to mind because I ate a few too many helpings at dinner tonight.)

Onward, then.

You need to have filed a Doing Business As (DBA) form as Big Oink Press with your local government so your business is official. After you've done that, you can get a checking account in the name of Big Oink Press. That isn't just convenient so you can track your business expenses and receipts. It's *required*. **Schools often are not allowed to write out a check for book purchases to an individual. It has to be to a company**. Do you want to get paid? File a DBA and set up your publishing checking account. (No, you don't have to incorporate. A sole proprietorship is fine.)

Provide a Professional Public Image for Your Company

If you're touting yourself as hot stuff, you don't want to look small potatoes. You want to look professional. Yes, Big Oink Press may publish only your books, and not even your mom will confuse it with a major New York house. But you want to look as professionally big-time as possible.

So you need a publishing website. It doesn't have to be elaborate, but you'll want it to include a way for a teacher to enter contact information so she can request an examination copy of your book. Ideally, that will be on its own page, so your promotional materials can point to it and it will be easy to find. Something like www.bigoinkpress.com/previewcopy. You might want to mention on that website page how quickly you'll be responding with an email so the teacher can check her Spam folder (or Gmail's "Promotions" tab) if she doesn't see anything in that time frame.

(It's beyond the scope of this book to get into website design, but if you've got a website, just search for a "contact plug-in" for your theme. Add that plug-in and configure it with the information you need. When a teacher fills out the form, the plug-in will send you an email with all the information.)

Ideally, you want a publishing email account or two. You'll list one of them along with the website information on your promotional materials so the teacher has two options for contacting you. It looks more professional for a teacher to correspond with schools@bigoinkpress.com than with whatever you use for your personal email (even though both of them are you).

Again, this is a matter of image, but image is important. Besides, most web hosting companies offer at least limited email for free. So along with your Big Oink Press website, you can set up a schools@bigoinkpress.com email account (and perhaps others), then set them to immediately redirect to your regular personal email so you don't have to check for mail in two places.

Since I prefer not to make it flagrantly obvious that my imprint carries only my titles—fair or not, many still view indie publishers with a jaundiced eye—I set the "display name" on my schools@bigoinkpress.com email account to my wife's maiden name. So when a teacher gets an email with download information and news that a print version of the book is on the way, she isn't getting it from someone named Hendrickson. As a result, I'm not blatantly announcing that I'm a one-man show, even though a casual glance at my publisher website makes it clear all the titles are by "David H. Hendrickson" and "D.H. Hendrickson." (Geez, I wonder if they're related?)

Using my wife's maiden name for email contact doesn't feel dishonest to me since she does just about everything possible to help me, including sending emails. We are a team in every sense of the word. I just don't want to rub a teacher's nose in the fact that I'm closer to small potatoes than really hot stuff. The illusion that I might be important isn't a bad one to foster, even if it's just little old me behind the curtain, like in *The Wizard of Oz*.

One last word of warning on email accounts. I would suggest using one like schools@bigoinkpress.com or publisher@bigoinkpress.com as opposed to promotions@bigoinkpress.com or marketing@bigoinkpress.com. The latter two seem more prone to their emails going into spam folders or Gmail's promotions tab.

Finally, all of this image building may not be absolutely required, but cut corners at your own risk.

CHAPTER 6

What's the Right Time for a Campaign?

Some campaigns are based on the hope a school will adopt your book for its students to read in the upcoming summer. Others are based on a teacher reading it herself during those same months, and recommending it for the students the following summer. Of course, sometimes you'll plan for one and get the other, but you want to play the percentages.

Campaigns Targeting the Upcoming Summer

The months of October and November are ideal when targeting the upcoming summer. January just barely squeaks by, but the further you get into a new calendar year, the more dependent you are on the teacher reading your book the minute she gets her hands on it. Here's why.

If the school year ends in mid-to-late June, you really need a purchase order in hand *at least* a month before that so you can place the order. (Many private schools get out almost a month earlier than those in the public sector, so be sure to factor that in, if appropriate.) If you make the time frame any tighter than a month, you're asking for trouble. Do you really want to risk the books arriving the day *after* the last day of school? Do you want to see a good chunk of your profit disappear if you have to pay potentially hundreds of dollars more for expedited shipping? Or two *thousand* dollars for priority shipping?

Additionally, if you're going to take advantage of the volume discounts available on very large orders—and good grief, you certainly should!—then you need to provide for the extra three weeks that CreateSpace requires on orders of at least one thousand copies, or the extra week IngramSpark typically requires for volume orders of 750 copies of a trade paperback or two thousand copies for hardcovers.

So if you're talking at least one thousand books at CreateSpace, you'll want the purchase order in hand *two* months before the end of the school year.

Working backward from there, I've seen it take almost two months from budget approval to seeing a purchase order. And although I haven't been privy to these particular conversations, I can imagine that a month or two could easily elapse from a teacher's recommendation until budget approval.

That means you really want your teacher or ELA chair going to bat for your book by January or February. Early March would be cutting it close, especially for a CreateSpace order of at least one thousand copies or an order to a private school. Any later could be too late.

(Of course, the time frame for getting your book added to an approved reading list is far more flexible and less rushed, but let's focus on the home run of an all-school read, if you can pull that off.)

To get the teacher making the recommendation by January or February, it's optimal to have the book in her hands during the months of October or November. Keep in mind that your book is *your* number one priority, but it isn't hers. She's got classes to prepare for and papers to correct, so it may not be until vacation weeks that she gets a chance to read it. It can still work if you're not getting the book to her until January, but she'll need to evaluate it quickly.

Campaigns Targeting a Future Year

For campaigns based on getting a teacher to read your book over her summer vacation and then recommend it for the following year, the months of January through mid-May are ideal. These months also work perfectly for the case of a school putting your book on a recommended reading list, but not actually buying copies for the students. Of course, schools will vary on when they decide on those lists, so the earlier the better.

So one can make a case for campaigns anytime from October through November as well as January through mid-May. Before we move on, though, let's complete the topic by explaining what's wrong with the other months. Obviously, nothing is worse than sending your flier to a teacher at her school address during the summer. Beyond that, avoid the first few weeks of the school year, perhaps all of September, because teachers are too caught up in the pandemonium of new students and new classes. Also avoid the last four weeks of the school year, because there's just too little time remaining to reliably get your promotional materials out, receive a request for a review copy, and then get a print copy to the reader before school closes.

Beyond those two bookends of the school year, you'll also want to avoid December. It's historically the worst time for direct mail campaigns. Like everyone else, teachers are busy that time of year, and they're getting barraged with advertising circulars and other holiday junk mail at home. Your promotional material isn't junk, and it'll be arriving at a school address, not at the teacher's home with all of the holiday advertising circulars, but it's all too natural for your decision maker to be in a default "chuck it" mentality.

CHAPTER 7

Electronic Review Copies or Paper?

When you contact schools, you'll be offering them complementary review copies of your book, or books. If you offer free print copies and do a large mailing, an overwhelmingly positive response could cost you hundreds of dollars. That's great, but you need to be prepared for it.

Let me provide a personal example. For my initial marketing campaign, I decided to target roughly three hundred schools with a two-page flier that mentioned two of my YA titles, *Offside* and *Cracking the Ice*. At the time, both were a bit longer than three hundred pages, so they cost me close to six dollars per copy from CreateSpace, shipping and tax included. Shipping one of them to a school via Media Mail, the cheapest form possible, pushes that to more than eight dollars per copy. If a school requested both books, I'd save a bit on shipping the two together, but I'd still be looking at fifteen dollars.

I believe in my books. I'm willing to bet on them—invest in them—to put them into decision makers' hands.

So if somehow sixty-seven of those teachers requested both books—an absurdly unrealistic number, but what if?—then I was willing to spend the thousand dollars it would take to give those books a chance.

I wasn't worried about freeloaders the way textbook publishers have to ferret out students posing as professors just to get a free book. I would know the identity of every school to which I sent promotional materials, and if somehow a request came in from some other source, it would be easy to determine if it were a legitimate school.

However, I did think of how in my younger years, I would request free samples of almost anything with no intent of ever making a purchase. Those book clubs that offered four books for a dollar with no obligation to ever buy anything got instant responses from me, and I inevitably bought nothing else from them. I was a freeloader, of sorts.

What if teachers with no actual interest in considering my book for adoption requested freebies with the sole intent of stocking their school libraries, not at all unlike my younger self? Having my books in school libraries is not a bad thing at all, but could I afford to finance that effort all across New England?

There was no book like this one to guide my way, and I wanted to keep my risks under reasonable control, so I initially promised electronic review copies in my promotional materials. Although I've since modified that stance for reasons I discuss below, it certainly is the approach to take if you're on a tight budget. And even if you choose to offer print copies, there's no reason not to at least have electronic copies as an option. You don't really want to lose out on an opportunity just because you couldn't be bothered to set up electronic distribution, do you?

You need to be able to deliver e-books to teachers in a way that is easy for them and doesn't erect any obstacles either for you or the teachers. I suggest bookfunnel.com. It has an entry-level plan for just twenty dollars a year that gives you more than what you need. My initial experience with them was as a reader, not a writer, and I thought their delivery of e-books was as seamless as possible. So set up an account there, or at some comparable provider, then upload the electronic versions of the books you want to distribute.

My original intent was to leave it at that. I promised an electronic review copy in my promotional materials and that's what I'd deliver. However, I altered my approach after a few teachers requested review copies, but then didn't download anything within the first few days. (BookFunnel lets you track this.) I was astounded at this development because, as I mentioned before, I can't imagine a better e-book delivery mechanism than BookFunnel.

Why would a teacher go to the trouble of entering contact information on my website, then not bother to download a copy? It didn't make sense. I now suspect my use of "promotions" for my imprint's email account at the time (promotions@pentucketpublishing.com) caused those emails to be derailed into Spam folders for the reasons mentioned in Chapter 5.

Whatever the case, I took no chances at losing a potential decision maker. I immediately sent the teacher a print copy. After all, I was getting a good response, but not one so overwhelming that the cost of paper copies would be exorbitant.

I've changed my approach so *I now provide both an electronic and a print copy for any teacher requesting a title*. Now, as soon as I get a teacher's request, I immediately respond with the download information, and say that a print copy is on its way. In my latest promotional materials, I don't even qualify the review copies as electronic. I want to minimize obstacles for teachers as decision makers. They'll get both versions.

I recommend you do the same. Just specify "a review copy," and if your response turns out to be so overwhelming that you can't afford the print cost, then at that point switch to electronic only. You'll have that flexibility.

Alternatively, you can add a checkbox to your website contact form where you ask for the teacher's preference, and then just provide the one version. For me, I like to send both.

Of course, if you're sending print copies, you need to make sure you have a reasonable number on hand as soon as requests come in. You don't want a teacher who is enthused about your book to lose that enthusiasm while you order copies from CreateSpace (because you're all out), get them shipped to you, then you ship a review copy to her.

Enthusiasm is valuable. Don't throw it away because you didn't stock up sufficiently. You don't need to keep a hundred or even fifty copies on hand. More like five or ten, depending on the size of your campaign. I prefer to have ten, then I order another ten if I drop down to five while a campaign is ongoing.

Of course, you could always drop-ship a copy to the teacher direct from CreateSpace in the same way you'll eventually handle an actual order. (This is discussed in Chapter 13.) But how impersonal is that? No letter from you to go with the book? That isn't putting your best foot forward. Have enough copies on hand that you can respond to requests and include a letter thanking the teacher for her interest.

If you need a rule of thumb, here it is. For every hundred schools you contact, have two copies available. (Chapter 9 will discuss where that number came from.) But always keep at least four or five on hand.

CHAPTER 8

Is There Such a Thing as Too Much Success? *Yes!*

DO NOT SKIP THIS CHAPTER!

You can destroy yourself financially if you don't sufficiently plan for success.

That may seem like an odd thing to say. After all, didn't I say way back in the first chapter that benefit number one can be the very nice payday from a school adopting your book? Am I talking out of both sides of my mouth?

No.

There's profit. Yay!

Then there's coping with cash flow problems. Yikes!

Let me explain, then give a personal example. Schools are *not* going to pay you up front for the books they buy from you. It isn't how they do business. If it was, every scam artist known to man would sell them a bill of goods, then disappear with the money. You may know that you're a saint who can be trusted with thousands of dollars, but the school doesn't.

Purchase Orders

The school will give you a purchase order. You deliver the books, then invoice the school for the books delivered. At some point after that—keep in mind the wheels of government grind slowly—you get paid.

In between you ordering those books from CreateSpace or IngramSpark—paying out of your own pocket—and the check arriving in the mail, you sweat financial bullets. For several months. Plan on at least three. (After which, your bank may add insult to injury by putting a partial hold on the check until it clears because of its size.)

You can specify on your invoice that the terms are net thirty days, but a government yawns at that. And forget trying to assess late fees. That would evoke laughter.

No one is trying to be mean or inconsiderate. It's just how the system works. I had my wife, who is an experienced professional at this kind of thing, nicely call a city's accounts department to inquire about its already well-overdue invoice. "Oh, yes, the books," the person on the other end of the line said. She knew of the order. "That's scheduled to be addressed in a meeting two weeks from now."

Just the way things work.

In that case, I paid over nine thousand dollars to CreateSpace, then waited three months before I got paid.

It was a wonderful payday. That check's arrival precipitated an awesome evening of celebration for myself and my wife.

But more than nine thousand dollars. Three months.

The good thing about governments (other than those rare cities teetering on bankruptcy) is that their purchase orders are considered solid. So with public schools, you shouldn't be worried about getting paid. But you must plan on delays.

(Please note that I'm not giving blanket guarantees for all public schools. I'm in no position to do that. Know whom you're doing business with. I'm just contrasting them with private schools, which have on occasion gone out of business and therefore should be scrutinized more closely, and with bookstores, which go out of business all the time. With bookstores, *always* insist on payment up front. A store's purchase order is too big a risk. But the unanimous opinion among all who I've spoken to in the industry is that public school purchase orders are as safe as you'll get.)

What if the very thought of nine-thousand-dollars-for-three-months makes you break into a cold sweat as the room spins wildly all about you? Or what if, worse than that, you simply couldn't pay CreateSpace that much money no matter how many cold sweats and spinning rooms you'd be willing to endure?

Give up?

No. You do have options. But I hope you understand now just how critical it is to do your planning in this area.

Cash Flow Options

If you're limited in terms of cash flow, see if your bank will extend a line of credit using a purchase order as collateral. See if you can loan money from your 401(k) in a timely manner. See if your rich Uncle Joe will front the money without forcing you to laugh at his lame jokes on Thanksgiving.

If the key people at the school know you personally—assuming that's a good thing, of course—offer a higher discount for payment up front. (Discounts are covered in Chapter 13.) I mentioned earlier in this chapter that it's too risky for a governmental agency to operate that way. But if you have a special relationship strong enough to possibly overcome that ironclad rule, it doesn't hurt to try.

Explore your options.

You can include an entry in your website's review copy request form that asks if the school typically purchases books for its students, the students buy the books, or both. That way before the teacher even gets a copy of your book, you've got a basic idea of what you're dealing with. You can begin to plan.

You can certainly run a smaller campaign, making a point to limit yourself to smaller schools with manageable-sized orders. That puts a ceiling on how many readers you can reach, and how much money you can make, but if that's what it takes, make that compromise. Perhaps you can use the profits from a small order this year to make your cash flow situation able to handle larger risks in the next campaign.

You can also opt to work with a distributor or a bookstore as an intermediary, as noted in Chapter 2, despite the disadvantages associated with that approach. You can choose to work only with those schools that will put your book on an approved reading list with the students all buying their own copies. No bulk orders through you.

Determine a plan that will work for you.

Plan for success.

CHAPTER 9

How Large of a Campaign Should You Run?

If you haven't read the previous chapter, go back and read it first. It's a prerequisite to everything we'll discuss here.

Done that? Okay, so you understand the potential cash flow land mines you're going to have to avoid, and you've assessed the level of exposure you can handle.

You've got a plan. Now, how many schools should you contact? How many are likely to respond?

Your response rate will depend on a number of factors, most notably the quality of your promotional materials. Did you catch the teacher's eye before she had a chance to toss your flier in the trash? Did you give her a reason to keep reading? Did you convince her that your book appears special enough to take the trouble of requesting a review copy?

We'll look at that topic in more detail in an upcoming chapter, but let's assume you produced a flier with quality content and a professional look. There's still an element of luck. Is the teacher opening your envelope on a good or a bad day? Is there something about your book that triggers good or bad thoughts and emotions based purely on that teacher's personal experiences? Does it have a special allure for that one teacher? Or the reverse?

There's a random element to all of this.

That said, for direct mail in general, a response rate of one to two percent is considered good. How does a campaign like the one you're considering compare to the industry average? Are you more or less likely to hit that figure?

My latest campaign ran a couple months before summer vacation. It targeted close to three hundred schools and generated requests from slightly more than three percent of them. Nine of those teachers responded. I hope to hit a higher percentage with an upcoming campaign, but for now, three percent works for me.

Will you be more or less likely to hit that figure? My two-page flier can point to all those Lynn English High School students loving my book and includes a glowing quote from the school's ELA chair. You may have a tough time matching that, but there may be aspects to your books that blow mine to smithereens. And I'm sure a lot of you are saying, "I *know* I'm smarter than that guy."

So pick a rough estimate of what you think your response rate might be. If you don't even have a foggy idea, start with that two-percent rule of thumb and go up or down based on your specific book and situation. Then combine that figure with the financial factors discussed in the last chapter. How much cash flow risk can you handle? That'll give you the *eventual* number of schools you should contact.

The First Time, Take a Staggered Approach

You're not going to send your promotional materials to all those schools at once. At least for your first campaign, I suggest sending your materials to a quarter of the number of schools you think you'll eventually contact. (So if you're going to target two hundred schools, start out with fifty.) Then wait two weeks and evaluate the feedback.

Teachers are almost always going to respond right away or close to it. The vast majority will toss your flier in the recycle bin. (Not the result you wanted, but at least they aren't using it for the teachers' lounge dart board.) We'll hope that a few teachers of exquisite taste send you an email or fill out the contact form on your website, and you're off and running. But only the worst of procrastinators will toss your flier on the desktop and say, "Ah, let me think about it for a few weeks."

Within two weeks, you'll have a pretty good idea of where you stand. If you're getting close to the return you expected, send out the next twenty-five to forty percent (fifty to eighty if your total was two hundred), then continue at that rate in the following weeks.

If, however, you're already getting flooded with requests, congratulations! You might want to cut back on the number of schools you were going to eventually contact. Drop from an eventual two hundred to only one hundred. At least slow down how many you send out this week. Perhaps send out only twenty-five this time. Remember the cash flow lessons of the last chapter, and don't overextend yourself. You can always use leftover materials in your *next* campaign.

On the other hand, if the silence is so deadly you can hear a pin drop, then do two things. Take another look at your promotional materials and make sure they're as good as they can be, then escalate your rate of sending them to schools. Plan to contact more schools than you originally projected.

This way you can tailor the size of your campaign to fit the level of success you can handle.

CHAPTER 10

Which Schools Should You Contact and How Do You Get Their Addresses?

If you're doing a very limited campaign of a small number of schools, you can probably get all the information you need from Google, if you don't know it already. That's particularly true for the specialized cases I mentioned in Chapter 4: schools of which you're an alum, or are in the city you live in, or are where your book is set.

Otherwise, especially if you're attempting a larger-sized campaign, you may find it's worth your while to purchase the contact information. For fifty dollars at high-schools. com, I purchased spreadsheets that include contact information for about 34,000 public and more than 9,000 private high schools. (Not all of those are exclusively high schools, but columns in the spreadsheets provide that information.) For those of you who are targeting younger readers, junior high schools are listed, and there's also a separate elementary school option.

You can download a sample before you decide whether or not to buy the entire database. You'll see there is not only the name, address, and phone number of the school, but also the total enrollment, breakdowns by gender, ethnicity, grade, and just about every possible criterion you could care about (though no email addresses), and plenty more besides. The private school spreadsheet contains information about religious affiliation, which a writer of inspirational fiction would find invaluable. The spreadsheets are based on 2012–2013 information for public schools and 2011–2012 for private, so there's the rare address change needed or a school that has been consolidated, but I found those to be less than one percent of the cases.

For me, this was a godsend. After archiving the original, I could reorganize the columns to ignore those I didn't care about (such as the number of hot lunches), and group together what mattered to me. I opted for higher enrollment schools, figuring they gave me the biggest bang for the buck, and I restricted myself (initially) to New England, since that's where I live and where the books are set.

I cut-and-pasted the school name and addresses into a document (from avery.com) that I then used to print mailing labels. Any school I sent my promotional materials to, I filled in with green in the spreadsheet so I'd know not to repeat in my next campaign (or I could repeat, knowing I was doing so).

Hey, if you've got the time and the inclination to look up all that information online (or at least all of it that you can find) for anything more than a small number of schools, knock yourself out. But does it really pass the WIBBOW test? I can't imagine that it does. Those spreadsheets saved a staggering number of hours and allowed me to target the most attractive schools.

CHAPTER 11

Creating Your Promotional Materials

There are entire books written about graphic design and use of powerful tools like InDesign. Those details are far beyond the scope of this book. Besides, if you're already designing your own covers, then you should have the tools and the basic expertise to handle the task yourself. If someone else designs your covers, the same almost certainly applies to her. What I hope to provide here are general guidelines that will help you, or your designer, create an eye-catching flier that contains the information a decision maker needs.

For starters, you need to limit yourself to no more than three pages, preferably only one or two. Anything more than that, and your promotional materials will instinctively feel to your audience like another term paper to correct. That's an insta-chuck into the trash. Probably with gusto.

Put yourself in an English teacher's shoes. She brings a stack of those often-wretched things home to correct on all too many nights. Plowing through them is most assuredly not the highlight of her life. If you provide her with what instinctively feels like yet another layer in her paper mountain of work, you're doomed.

Your flier shouldn't look like a term paper either. Beneath a catchy headline, it should include a large cover image of your book. Preferably in color. Yes, you can save money going black-and-white (more on that in the next chapter), but your campaign will live and die based on your ability to catch the teacher's eye. Color images help you with that, but unless you're going for a noir look for your book, black-and-white won't.

The text can't be rambling paragraphs—it'll be the pull quotes or the active sales copy (i.e., the blurb) you already use to sell the book on retailer websites.

Easy to read. Eye-catching. Professional.

I don't pretend to be perfect, but you can see my own two-page flyer on the Web Supplements page at pentucketpublishing.com. Is it easy to read, eye-catching, and professional? I'd like to think so. Design your own materials to achieve those same goals.

The key is to think like that English teacher. You put yourself into your point-of-view characters' heads all the time. Now, put yourself into the teacher's head. What is it about your book that will catch her eye? What is it that she'll find interesting? What makes it different—*and better for her and her students*—than all the others out there?

You believe in your book, don't you? Let her know why.

No passive sentences. No rambling description of plot.

It's an advertisement for your book! Sound excited about it! You've got a second or two of this teacher's attention before she chucks your flier. Hook her in that second or two, and she'll give you a few more seconds. Fail to hook her, and you're gone.

On the bottom of the page (or one of the pages if you've got more than one), use two or three inches of vertical space to provide directions for ordering a review copy, much like I did in my own flyer. As noted above, you can see it on the Web Supplements page at pentucketpublishing.com.

When you're finished with your design, be sure to generate the highest resolution output possible. That's typically a setting in your design tool. You want the text and images to look sharp and crisp to maximize their professional appearance and instinctive appeal.

CHAPTER 12

How to Drive Your Costs Down

There are two types of costs to consider. First, the cost of your marketing campaign. Second, the cost of your book if a school adopts it. The latter offers by far the greatest potential for savings, but let's look at the marketing costs first.

Reducing the Cost of Your Campaign

My suggestion is that you do *not* try to save pennies that might make your promotion appear anything less than one-hundred-percent professional. Don't be penny wise and pound foolish.

First impressions matter.

For example, you could skip the cost of envelopes and merely staple your folded flier together and mail it that way. But doesn't that look cheap? Doesn't that make your flier something that more instinctively belongs in the trash? How do you react when something like that arrives in your mail? Envelopes cost little and provide a more professional looking presentation.

Similarly, you can pinch pennies by forgoing mailing labels and writing the addresses on the envelopes by hand. But doesn't a computer-generated mailing label look more professional?

The absolute worst attempt at economy, however, is to use your own printer for the photocopying of your promotional materials if it doesn't produce high-quality, high-resolution copies. And a corollary to this is opting for a black-and-white flier instead of color just to save on copying cost.

The quality of your flier—both its content and appearance—will decide the fate of your campaign. Don't stack the deck against yourself by trying to economize in this most critical area. It is the worst example of being penny wise and pound foolish.

Yes, I got sticker shock when I went to my local Staples and found out how much it charged for color copies. I needed 300 copies of my two-page flier. I recoiled at the number, then looked for alternatives. I found PrintDirtCheap.com, and got those 600 total pages for $101, shipping included, which amounts to less than seventeen cents per copy. And the quality was great.

Do not compromise the physical appearance of your promotional materials.

There are, however, ways that you can save. If a postage rate increase is looming, stock up on Forever stamps. It's a small savings but an easy one to achieve. You can buy your envelopes in bulk or get good prices at places like the Dollar Store.

Reducing the Cost of Your Book

Your biggest savings—*dramatic savings*—can come in reducing the cost of the book itself. In general, CreateSpace offers the lowest cost per book (compared to Lightning Source and IngramSpark) until you hit 750 copies, and there are none of the other two companies' setup or handling charges. Lightning Source and IngramSpark, however, become the best option for quantities of at least 750 copies when applying their volume discounts. (We'll look at those details in the next chapter.) And even at lower quantities, those two companies offer a cheaper shipping option called "Economy Heavyweight" that can override their higher per-book costs.

The variables are too numerous to enumerate here. Your best bet is to use the print cost calculators at each site using the specifics for your own book and see the results for various quantities.

Another alternative once you have an order in hand is to consider a local offset printer. A friend of mine has enjoyed excellent success with this approach, driving down her book's cost dramatically while achieving the same quality. A little research could pay big dividends.

Regardless of who prints your book, however, you should first look at its layout to see if you can reduce page count. My own book, *Offside*, was originally laid out with a blank page whenever a chapter was going to begin on the left-facing page. This is hardly a requirement. Some books published by the largest houses follow this approach; others do not. If your book has forty chapters, opting to skip the blank pages will cut your page count down by about twenty. Perhaps your chapters begin with some excess blank lines that can be trimmed or some of your chapters end with just a few lines of text. Some judicious changes in the kerning and leading can make dramatic differences without affecting the quality at all.

Do not compromise quality! Don't make the font so small or the layout so visually unappealing that a reader takes one look at the page and subconsciously recoils, or at least begins to feel tired. Maintain a pleasing appearance to each page no matter what.

In the case of *Offside*, however, the changes by my layout wizard, Dayle Dermatis, dropped the page count from 302 to 240. My jaw dropped at that astounding result. I had to flip through the output, even though I trust Dayle implicitly, and see it myself to believe it. And the book still looked awesome! (In case you're wondering, she can be found at dayledermatis. com, but she is not taking on additional clients. She is, however, a wonderful writer, and I highly recommend her books.)

See the Web Supplements page at pentucketpublishing. com for a before-and-after look of a sample chapter. Your own page-reduction efforts may fall a bit short of that gold standard, but those changes can make a major difference.

My per-book cost of *Offside* plummeted from $4.47 to $3.73, a whopping savings of 74 cents. For an order of 1000 copies (before factoring in volume discounts), that's a savings of $740!

It will cost you, either in your time if you do your own layout, or in paying your designer, to make the changes. You'll also need to tweak your cover to account for the thinner spine. But as you can see, the payoff is dramatic. (And you'll certainly opt for making those design choices right from the outset for future books.)

Of course, there are no guarantees you'll hit the big pay-day to pay off that redesign. At least not right away. Maybe not ever.

Redesign Now or Later?

You can gamble and redesign for the lower cost, knowing you might not recoup your investment. Or you can wait for a deal that will pay for the redesign. The latter is certainly the safer route financially, but it does have its drawbacks. Will there be enough time for you or your designer to do the work, get it submitted to CreateSpace (or its alternatives), check out the proof copies, and then order the real copies? (Under no circumstances should you just "wing it" and make a large order without having actually examined a proof copy. If there's some mistake or oversight, it's your fault because you would have caught it in the proof. The school isn't going to accept those defective copies. You'll be stuck with them and on the hook for their cost.)

The other negative to waiting on the redesign is that a school might feel you pulled a bait-and-switch giving them a 302-page review copy (using the *Offside* example), and then delivering one that weighs in at only 240 pages. They might even assume that it's an abridged version and you're pulling a fast one on them. This situation can be salvaged, but you'll need to be up front about the redesign and be clear that every single word is there, and you've done that work so that you can offer the attractive discounts you've promised.

Just don't whistle past this graveyard, saying nothing, and think the school won't notice.

By the way, there is one other hidden benefit to reducing the page count. Reluctant readers will reflexively choose a 240-page book over one that tops 300 pages. All schools have at least some of these readers, especially, it seems, among the boys. So if your title isn't mandatory reading but rather is on a list with many other alternatives, the page reduction can make your book more attractive to those readers.

CHAPTER 13

The Financial Nitty-Gritty: Discounts and Profit Margins

So how much of a discount can you offer schools? How much will you make on the deal?

There's a healthy dollop of math in this chapter, but it's really all just simple arithmetic. Not as bad as it looks, if you're math-phobic. I'll try to simplify and summarize as often as possible.

Your Printing and Shipping Costs

First, let's look at your printing and shipping cost. To make the calculations easy, we'll begin using only CreateSpace numbers and assume the school needs 1000 copies. That quantity is actually where significant volume discounts kick in, but we'll factor those in later in this chapter. For now, we just want to keep the example as clear and simple as possible. We'll use my book, *Offside*, in its 302-page incarnation before the layout design dropped its page count so dramatically.

For a book of that length, CreateSpace charges $4.47 per copy. Both Lightning Source and IngramSpark charge more until you get to their volume discounting at 750 copies (though they do offer one super-cheap shipping option), so we'll stick with CreateSpace for now. At $4.47 per copy, that's $4,470 for 1000 of them. Standard shipping for that many books costs $403. (Expedited shipping would be $810, and priority shipping a whopping $2,013. See why you don't want to get too close to the last day of school before you finish the deal?)

What about the shipping costs you face getting the books to the school after CreateSpace ships them to you? You aren't going to be incurring those costs. You'll tell CreateSpace to drop ship those copies direct to the school. You're never going to touch them. On the order page where you'd usually be specifying your own address, you'll specify the school's shipping address, as specified on its purchase order. It's easy, and companies like CreateSpace drop ship packages all the time. Besides, do you really want to have to physically handle those 1000 copies, first on the receiving end and then shipping?

Sales Tax

Now we need to talk sales tax.

Sales tax, you ask? But public schools and many private ones are tax exempt. They don't pay sales tax.

That's true. But you do. Unless your publishing entity is also tax exempt, you have to pay sales tax.

Well, maybe.

That issue was a stunner to me when placing the order for Lynn English High School. An almost $500 stunner. Money out of my pocket.

Of course, sales tax laws vary on a state-by-state basis, so you'll need to research the specifics of where your publishing entity is based and also the school's state, if that's different. Just be aware that for many states, CreateSpace will collect sales tax from you regardless of the school's non-exempt status. That is its default position, and if you ask Customer Service, you'll likely assume its explanation means you have no choice but to swallow the cost.

Not true.

Depending on the state, you may have an important option, even assuming that your publishing entity is not itself tax-exempt. In a situation like this, your imprint is a reseller of the books that CreateSpace is printing. If your publishing entity acquires from your state a Uniform Sales and Use Tax Certificate and Reseller Certificate, then it qualifies as a reseller that is itself responsible for collecting sales tax. So as long as you file the appropriate paperwork with CreateSpace (and give it a week to process), then you may not be on the hook for the sales tax as long as the school is in that same state. (If your school is in another state, then you may be out of luck anyway.) Put simply, you will have shifted the burden of collecting the sales tax from CreateSpace to your imprint, and your imprint won't have to collect from a tax-exempt school.

Before, however, you rush off to file for such a reseller certificate with your state Department of Revenue, be sure you know what you're signing up for. If the only books you (or your publishing entity) are actually selling direct to a customer are to a handful to friends—sales that can be considered as personal use—then there's something to be said for leaving the sales tax to CreateSpace.

As soon as you've acquired that reseller certificate, you're not only required to collect the sales tax from non-exempt customers, you're also required to file sales tax returns *even if you've collected no tax*. Depending on the state, that may be as often as monthly. That requirement continues as long as you're a reseller. I know of one person who had to file those returns every month for eighteen months after his father died because there was the potential of a sale of equipment. Monthly filings of zero collected tax. And if it wasn't in by the due date of the 20th, a notice arrived on the 24th.

Again, every state is different. Do your homework, and do it up front. Be informed and then make an informed decision. Don't get blindsided like I did the first time with no time to consider alternatives. And if you do pay the sales tax, be sure to point it out to your accountant at income tax time. In fact, talk to your accountant ahead of time so you handle it in the most efficient way possible. There may even be advantages to setting up two business entities, one with the reseller certificate and one without.

Adding Up the Costs

Okay, let's move onward. Let's assume you either don't have a reseller's certificate or it doesn't apply because the school is in another state, one where CreateSpace collects sales tax. Or perhaps it's to a private school that isn't tax exempt. So for our hypothetical 1000-book order, let's factor in $327 for sales tax. (It's a quirky number, but it gets our total cost to a nice, round number.)

Adding that to the printing and shipping costs mentioned at the start of this chapter brings our total cost to a nice even $5200, or $5.20 per book. All of those variables will be slightly different with your book. The per-book cost will vary according to its length, its color interior instead of black and white, and whether you're using CreateSpace or an alternative printer. The shipping cost per book will go up by a few pennies on a smaller order (43 cents for 100 books, compared to 40.3 cents for 1000), or go down for a larger one. And the sales tax depends on your state. But $5.20 per book gives us a close approximation.

Or to summarize (for 1000 copies):

Printing	4,470
Shipping	403
Sales Tax	327
Total	5,200
Per Book	5.20

Volume Discounts

Now let's talk about volume discounts. They start at 1000 copies at CreateSpace, and 750 for trade paperbacks at IngramSpark and Lightning Source. (Until late in 2017— just before this book went to press, don't you know?—the volume discounting at the latter two sources didn't start until 2000 copies. This lower threshold may have forced some deadline scrambling on my part, but is outstanding news for all of us.)

I'll cut to the chase. **The per-book pricing at quantities below 750 are lower at CreateSpace** (aside from shipping cost differences). **The per-book pricing from 750 on up are lower at IngramSpark and Lightning Source**, where they are identical to each other.

However, many writers have their titles only at CreateSpace, so we'll still look at the details there. See the chart below, however, to see how dramatic of a cost difference there can be. You may decide it's time to get your titles in IngramSpark (or Lightning Source).

This isn't hard. Just be aware that you need to opt out of CreateSpace's Extended Distribution, and your book also needs an ISBN that you did *not* get from CreateSpace. If you bought your ISBN through CreateSpace, whether it was a free one that lists the imprint as CreateSpace or the since-discontinued version that cost ten dollars that allowed you to list it under your own imprint, you'll need a new ISBN (and an interior that reflects that change) for your version at IngramSpark (or Lightning Source).

Onward, then, to the details.

At CreateSpace, you'll get a 20-percent discount on purchases from 1000–1499 copies, a 30-percent discount from 1500–1999, and a 35% discount on those of 2000 and above. *This discount is not automatically applied to your order. If you don't call and ask for it from Customer Service, you won't get it.* In fact, its availability is hidden on the website, basically making it a secret. It also requires an *extra* three weeks printing time, so if you're a month away from summer vacation, you're too late. That said, if your deadline for delivery warrants it and your title is only with CreateSpace, contact Customer Service first—do *not* fill out the usual order form—and proceed from there.

These discounts would drop the per-book printing cost of our example from $4.47 to $3.58 (20 percent off) or to $3.13 (30 percent off) or to $2.91 (35 percent off). The discounts also apply to any sales tax you might be paying, since you'd pay tax on a lower total, but do not affect shipping. So our hypothetical $5.20 total per-book cost would drop to $4.25, $3.76, and $3.53 for the three categories of volume discounts.

At IngramSpark and Lightning Source, the volume discount can become enormous. The discount isn't hidden the way it is at CreateSpace; you just select the "Volume Service" option that isn't shown until you hit the 750-copy threshold. You need to allow for extra printing time, but not much; typically an extra five business days. The per-book cost of our 302-page example drops to $2.97 at 750 copies and plummets all the way to $1.59 at 3000 copies.

Per-Book Cost (Before Shipping and Tax)

Quantity	CreateSpace	Lightning Source	IngramSpark
Up to 750	4.47	4.50 to 5.42	4.83
750–999	4.47	2.97	2.97
1000–1499	3.58	2.57	2.57
1500–1999	3.13	2.57	2.57
2000–2999	2.91	1.92	1.92
3000+	2.32	**1.59**	**1.59**

Perhaps that's all just a blur of numbers for you. If so, let me illustrate it this way. *A 1290-copy order at IngramSpark using Volume Service costs less than a conventional order of 700 copies. Not less per book. A lower total cost, even including low-cost shipping of the extra books* ($3,529 vs. $3,526, including shipping, excluding tax).

The extra 590 copies are free!

You can't mix-and-match titles, such as asking for 500 of one book and 500 of another. You also can't split the destination where the books are shipped, such as 500 to a school and 500 to your house. Volume discounts at both IngramSpark and CreateSpace are for one title and one shipping address.

But the magnitude of that discount—*hundreds of copies are free!*—should set off alarm bells of opportunity for you. If you have time to ship the books twice, ship the volume-discount number of copies to yourself, then send only the required number to the school. Yes, you'll be paying the shipping cost to get them from you to the school, but it'll be worth it. Or, if the school is convenient, and you or someone you can depend on can deliver the books by hand, do it! Rent a truck and dolly so you don't hurt your back doing any heavy lifting. For one day, you have formed the *I Ain't Broke No More* delivery service. Or if your relationship with the school allows it, have the full allotment of books sent to the school with the understanding that you'll collect the excess. Explain that this helps you give them an excellent discount.

Of course, be sure you let whomever you share your living space with know that there may be 500 copies (or whatever the number may be) stacked in boxes for quite some time. Your partner may not be amused, especially if space is tight. Your landlord might even point out that it's a violation of your lease. So do your due diligence up front.

That said, if you can pull it off, how great will it be if your next deal could be filled using free copies stacked in your storage space? That, my friends, is taking the "driving your costs down" mentality to a most wonderful pinnacle.

We'll proceed from this point on to ignore volume discounts, except parenthetically. That's to keep examples as simple as possible, and keep those who are math-phobic from slamming their heads on the table. But I hope this section has illustrated the magnitude of an impact these discounts can provide.

List Price and Discounts

Your profit will depend on your book's list price and the discount you offer. The higher the list price, the more flexibility you have with discounting while maintaining a strong profit margin. However, higher list prices provide a barrier to other sales of that book, including cases where a school isn't buying copies, but instead putting you on a recommended reading list. A list price of $18.99 for a CreateSpace trade paperback is more of a barrier than one set at $12.99.

Let's look at three list price points—$12.99, $15.99, and $18.99—and also at three discount levels—40, 45, and 50 percent. To simplify matters, I'm going to assume that each of those discounts *also* include free shipping. If you don't want to do that, then add 40 cents extra profit for each book, or $403 total extra profit for our theoretical 1000 book order. (If you're paying sales tax, don't even think about trying to pass that on to a public school. They know they don't pay sales tax; if you have to as part of this deal, that's *your* problem. Don't even bring it up.)

Onward to the math.

If you multiply the list price times 0.6 (for a 40-percent discount) times 0.55 (for 45 percent) and times 0.5 (for 50 percent), and then subtract your cost of $5.20 per book, you get the following values for the per-book profit, assuming free shipping.

Per-Book Profit, Based on Discounts

List Price	50%	45%	40%
12.99	1.30	1.94	2.59
15.99	2.80	3.59	4.39
18.99	4.30	5.24	6.19

If numbers make your eyes glaze over, all of the above simply means that your 1000-copy order nets your $12.99 book a total profit ranging from $1,300 to $2,590, depending on the discount. If your book instead lists for $15.99, the total profit ranges from $2,800 to $4,390. And if it lists for $18.99, then the range goes from $4,300 to $6,190.

Take the specifics for your own title, tweak the numbers, and figure out the discount that makes sense for you. Don't feel that the above discounts are the only ones you can use. If you can only offer a 25-percent discount, then use those numbers. Perhaps the discount will depend on the size of the order: one level for smaller orders, another for medium-sized ones, and yet another for those that qualify you for the volume discounts discussed in the previous section (but be sure to specify a requirement for a sufficient lead time). If you want to keep something in reserve for the case where you might have to negotiate, then don't initially offer free shipping, but add it if needed.

Strike a balance between offering a good deal and giving yourself an appropriate reward for your efforts, both the writing and the marketing, and also for dealing with a major cash flow headache for three or four months. Don't sell yourself short.

If You Use a Distributor

Finally, let's contrast doing the order fulfillment yourself with what happens if the order goes through either a distributor or a bookstore (which also uses a distributor), as discussed in Chapter 2. For comparison's sake, we'll assume you would have given a 40-percent discount with free shipping had you done the deal direct.

Your $12.99 book will earn only 72 cents per book under CreateSpace's Extended Distribution. To my mind, that's not sufficient compensation for your writing and marketing efforts. You supposedly hit it big with a 1000-copy sale, but your profit didn't make it out of the triple digits. Instead of the $2,590 profit on a direct sale, you made $720, less than 28 cents on the dollar.

The numbers are better if you use IngramSpark. There, you set the wholesale discount you are offering, which then determines the discount Ingram's customers, such as bookstores and perhaps the schools you are targeting, will get. The recommendation there is that you set your discount at 55 percent so that Ingram's customers will get the discount they are accustomed to, which in a typical case would be 40 percent, with a bit more for larger orders, say 43 percent. The difference is what Ingram takes as its profit (roughly 15 percent) as the distributor.

At a 55 percent wholesaler discount, however, you are only making $1.02 per book. The 39.5 cents on the dollar is better than CreateSpace's 28 cents, but still a far cry from if you sold the books directly.

For you to get a sufficient return on your efforts when using a distributor, one of two things must happen. First, you need to raise the list price. If you went from $12.99 to $15.99, that would give you a $1.92 profit through CreateSpace's Extended Distribution, and a $2.37 profit through IngramSpark when using a 55-percent wholesaler discount. The downside to raising your list price, of course, is that a higher price poses more of a barrier to other sales.

The alternative is to forget about CreateSpace Extended Distribution, which you should do anyway because IngramSpark offers a better deal. Use CreateSpace only for sales to Amazon and to yourself. Opt out of Extended Distribution.

Then go with a lower wholesale discount on IngramSpark than 55 percent. At 50 percent, you'll make $1.66 per book on your $12.99 title, and at 45 percent, you'll make $2.31. Personally, I think you should make at least two dollars per book. But who am I to say? I'm using direct sales. You are the boss.

The downside to going below a 55-percent wholesale discount is that Ingram will still take its 15-percent cut. It isn't in business to finance your profit margins. This means that its customers who would be expecting roughly a 40-percent discount instead will be looking at something closer to 30 percent. If bookstores are already carrying your titles, this would be a problem. They could drop you like a hot potato.

Most indie writers that I know, however, sell very little through these channels. Unless you're an exception, set the wholesaler discount that works for you. As long as your school has an Ingram account, it will be able to order your title through that channel and you'll have none of the cash flow issues discussed earlier. The school will be getting a lower discount than it expects, but you can explain that you are small publishing house that has chosen to go for low list prices at the expense of their usual expected discount.

If You Use a Bookstore

If the school does not have an Ingram account, your odds of a deal just dropped. You'll have to find a bookstore willing to work with you despite a lower than expected discount for itself. That might be a tough sell, because most small bookstores can no more handle cash flow problems than you can. And if the bookstore is getting squeezed on its discount, it's not going to be able to offer much one to the school.

And if the school has to pay close to list price for all those copies, it may not be able to fit your book into its budgetary requirements or the ceiling on its grant.

All of which is why I prefer selling direct to schools. I know the cash-flow problem can be a scary one, but consider my suggestion about getting a short-term business loan using the purchase order as collateral. Banks are in business to make low-risk loans just like that. Don't give up on selling direct too quickly.

If you can't do it, however, I suggest going through Ingram at a discount that gets you at least two dollars a book, then make it clear after teachers begin requesting your book how you'll need to proceed.

CHAPTER 14

What About Hardcovers?

What if a school requests a hardcover edition of your book? It's best to be prepared.

You and I might view the current cost of print on demand hardcovers as prohibitive. You'll need to price yours at about twice the cost of your trade paperback. That isn't going to sell many copies to the general public, but a school might view things differently.

To a great extent, it all comes down to how a school intends to use your book. If it's going to be used a single time by just one student over the course of a summer, then the economy of a trade paperback is the obvious choice. The same holds true for a private school in which the students purchase their own books.

If, however, your book is intended for ongoing use, semester after semester, such as in an AP English class, then the durability of a hardcover suddenly becomes attractive, even at a high price.

Hardcover Options

So what are your options? You've got one, or more accurately, two flavors of the same option: Lightning Source and IngramSpark. Both companies operate under the same corporate umbrella, and they offer hardcovers while CreateSpace does not. (You may also want to consider a local offset printer as yet another option.)

A school can choose between a "cloth" cover, with or without a dust jacket, and "case laminate," a color-laminated cover glued to boards with no dust jacket. My first novel was sold to a traditional YA publisher that exclusively used case laminate with a glossy finish because of its durability, and I suspect schools will make the same choice. We'll use that for our examples. If you choose a cloth cover, the cover itself costs the same, but the jacket will cost roughly an extra dollar.

You will need to do some redesign of your CreateSpace trade paperback cover because the specifications are different. So budget for that task from both a cost and time perspective.

As with trade paperbacks, IngramSpark hardcovers cost the same, regardless of quantity, until the magical Volume Discount kicks in, whereas Lightning Source copies begin at a higher cost and drop gradually based on quantity.

Doing the Math

Let's look at the cost of the 302-page example we've used up to this point. IngramSpark charges $9.39 per book (plus shipping and possible sales tax) for all quantities through

1999 copies. Lightning Source, on the other hand, uses a sliding scale.

With trade paperbacks, we saw these two vendors offer volume discounts starting at 750 copies. For hardcovers, they don't kick in until you hit 2000 copies, but the discounts are staggering.

Hardcover Per-Book Cost (Before Shipping and Tax)

Quantity	Lightning Source	IngramSpark
Up to 100	9.85	9.39
100–199	9.75	9.39
200–299	9.16	9.39
300–399	8.96	9.39
400–499	8.67	9.39
500–749	8.17	9.39
750–999	7.88	9.39
1000–1999	7.48	9.39
2000–2999	**2.61**	**2.61**
3000+	**2.32**	**2.32**

Those last two rows are not typos. From a $9.39 per-book cost at IngramSpark and $7.48 at Lightning Source, the cost plummets to $2.61 for 2000 copies and $2.32 for 3000. Yes, that does mean that 6000 copies using Volume Service costs more than a thousand dollars *less* than 1999 copies using the standard Economy Service. This is presumably because of the ability to use highly economical web presses at high volumes.

If you can generate those kinds of quantities, then you're home free. But let's assume you're talking numbers more like

300 copies (a Lightning Source cost of $8.96). For ease of discussion, let's use $9.00 per book and 1000 copies, while recognizing that your cost will be lower as long as your quantities are at least 200 and you're using Lightning Source.

So that's $9,000 for the printing, $50 handling, $203 for shipping, and an overly generous allowance of $747 for sales tax to get the total cost to an even $10,000.

If you price your hardcover at $24.99 and offer a 40-percent discount with free shipping, you'll collect $14,994 for a profit of $4,994. At a discount of 50 percent with free shipping, you'll still be making $2,495. And both those profit figures are low because I inflated the per-book cost and the sales tax to make for an easy illustration.

Going Through a Distributor

What if you sell that same $24.99 book through the IngramSpark distribution channel at a 55-percent wholesale discount? Your profit is $1.86 per book (or $1,860 for 1000 copies). At a 50-percent discount, the per-book profit becomes $3.10, and at 45 percent, it grows to $4.35. The same issues associated with this option that were discussed in the previous chapter apply here as well.

In summary, you'll need to set the list price of your hardcover at about twice that of the trade paperback, but it may still be an option schools are interested in. Ideally, you'll be prepared to offer it to them.

PART III: RESULTS!

From Campaign to Champagne

CHAPTER 15

Your Campaign Begins and Review Copy Requests Come In

By now, you've got everything in place. You're probably ready to explode with anticipation or collapse from exhaustion. Either way, you're tired of planning. You just want results.

Enough of the foreplay. Let's get on with the action.

So you tuck your promotional page or pages into an envelope, preferably using a mailing label for the school and one with a return address for your publishing entity. As mentioned in Chapter 9, you may be breaking down your mailings into two-week intervals, or just going for broke.

What do you do now?

Write your next book until the requests for review copies come in. In fact, I'm hoping that all through this process, you've kept writing. Maintaining a balance between writing and publishing can be difficult, but it's essential.

If no requests come in, don't give up too quickly. Remember that a one- or two-percent response rate is a good one for direct mail campaigns in general. This may be a tougher nut than average to crack. Be sure your promotional materials are as effective as possible, then keep sending them to more schools until you either do get requests or you've exhausted the budget you established for the campaign. If it's the latter, only you can decide whether it's worth another try in the future, perhaps with a different book or books, or approaching the promotional materials from a different angle, or targeting different schools. I hope you arrive on a winning combination.

If, on the other hand, requests come in, then how do you respond?

You email from your version of a schools@bigoinkpress.com account. Use a subject line specific to your book (something like "Your requested copy of *My Awesome Novel*") so it doesn't look like spam. Thank the teacher for her interest, specify the BookFunnel download link or links for immediate access, and as long as you're providing print review copies, say that one will be in the mail in the next day or two.

Here's an example that uses my own book titles.

Dear Teacher Name,

Thank you for your interest in Cracking the Ice*! We'll get you a print copy in the mail immediately.*

We also use a service called BookFunnel that makes it easy for you to download a digital copy to any device. If you have any trouble, just tap the Help Me link at the top of the book download page and their friendly support team will help you get your copy. If you still have any problems, just let us know. We'll fix it.

For Cracking the Ice, *click here or paste the following into your browser: https://dl.bookfunnel.com/*

fillinyourlink. If you'd also like to preview Offside, *click here or paste the following into your browser: https:// dl.bookfunnel.com/fillinyourlink*

If you decide to adopt either title for your students to read, please let us know. If your school purchases books for the students, we accept purchase orders and offer substantial bulk discounts.

Again, thank you for your interest. Let us know if you have any questions or concerns.

Sincerely,
Your Publishing Contact Name

You might want to use Priority Mail (the flat rate envelope) for sending print copies, depending on the geography and time of year. You may be close enough to the school to make the speed difference between Priority Mail and Media Mail negligible. But beware the December holidays. Media Mail is the cheapest way to ship for a reason. It gets lowest priority when it comes to loading the trucks. After the first week or so in December, spend the money on Priority Mail. It also sends a positive subconscious message to the teacher that she is a priority of your company. Decide for yourself if the benefits are worth the cost.

Although that teacher will primarily be focused on the quality of your book and how well it suits the school's needs, it's a good idea to drop a hint about the financials. She'll likely have at least some idea of the budgetary allotment on purchase orders or a grant ceiling for purchasing a required book. So specify that significant bulk discounts are available, and if you don't display the list price on your book cover, be sure to include that information, too. If you offer hardcovers, mention that option.

It doesn't hurt to suggest that the teacher put your email account in a "not spam" folder to make sure there aren't missed communications. I recommend that you ask when the teacher would like you to get back to her with further details. It's your call as to whether you do this, but I like the idea of getting some message back from a teacher, even if it's "Don't call us, we'll call you." You're not going to want to be a pest and kill your prospects by being annoying. If the teacher responds, you'll know the date to put on your calendar for your next email. And if she doesn't, be aware that your email may have gone into a spam folder or Gmail's Promotions tab and hasn't been seen.

If you get nothing back, wait a few weeks, then send an email saying you just wanted to make sure the print copy arrived. If you still hear nothing, *send the same message via conventional mail.* A stamp and an envelope is cheap. A lost opportunity can cost thousands.

CHAPTER 16

A School is Interested!

You get an email that the school is interested. Yay! You're not past the finish line, but you can see it. You can smell it.

Don't go and spend your profits yet. There are still hurdles to be cleared and, as I noted in Chapter 12, your finances might actually be tight for several months until payment actually arrives. But you're ninety percent of the way there.

Now for that last ten percent.

Closing Details

Your contact person may change now, perhaps from the English teacher who has recommended your book to the principal. Whatever the case, if your previous email didn't mention a specific discount, then here is where you get into the details. Your contact tells you how many books and by what date they're needed, and you indicate the discount and how it all adds up to a final total. If you are not providing free shipping, be sure to add that to the total cost. There can't be any last-minute surprises for the school.

At the same time, you don't want any last-minute surprises either. Specifically say that a component of the strong discount you're providing is that there are no returns. Once the purchase order is finalized, you'll "authorize the print run" based on that fixed number of copies. After all, you don't want a couple hundred books stacked in your apartment because the school returned them, expecting a credit. Defective copies will, of course, be replaced, but extras can't be returned.

That shouldn't be an issue. Purchase orders are there to specify exact numbers. So you don't need to beat the issue into the ground. Just mention it up front, and when it comes time to send an invoice, you can list it there, too.

Also, if you're getting close to the end of the school year, be clear about when you need the purchase order to be able to deliver the books on time. This is especially important if you're giving CreateSpace an extra three weeks to print the books based on their volume discount.

By the way, don't be bashful about making clear how good a deal the school is getting, how much it's saving. Using our $12.99 book, 1000 copy, 40-percent discount with free shipping example, say that with shipping it would have cost $13,393, but after discount it's only $7,794, a savings of $5,599! That's a great deal. Say so.

With any luck, it all goes smoothly from here. But what if your contact (let's say it's the principal from this point on) tries to negotiate? All your numbers should be easily accessible for you. You did all the calculations back when deciding on the discount in the first place. If you deliberately held something in reserve for negotiations—something like free shipping—it may be an easy call.

If, however, the principal's demand is something you need to think about, just say that you aren't authorized to make that decision and you'll get back to her. If it's so outrageous that you wouldn't possibly accept it, decline in a nice way— "I'm sorry, but we couldn't do that"—but don't give up. See if there's something you can do to salvage the deal. Take a shot.

On the other hand, let's say the school's grant is for $7,500 and you're $294 over her limit. She isn't nickel-and-diming you; she's got a hard limit. Are you going to throw away a profit of $2,296 because it was supposed to be $2,590 and you won't budge?

I wouldn't. I'd write back that her case warrants an exception and Big Oink Press will accommodate that request. At the very least, you should respond, "I think we can make that exception, but let me get it confirmed." Then within an hour, provide the confirmation.

Even after all of that discussion, however, it may take some time before you get your purchase order. Until it arrives, you don't order the copies, because nothing is certain.

You'll be asked to fill out a W-9 form for your publishing entity. That's no big deal, something that shouldn't take more than five minutes after you download the form from the IRS, but you should be aware of one detail. If you always use a post office box for Big Oink Press, you'll want to use a street address for the W-9, and that's likely the same address where your check will eventually be mailed. There isn't total unanimity on this point, but the IRS says on forms like the 1040 that you should specify a street address, not a post office box, unless the street address cannot receive mail.

I never like to impose obstacles to a deal so even though I always use a PO box for my own publishing entity, I use my street address on the W-9. And that's where the check arrives.

Beyond that, it's all a waiting game for the purchase order.

The Purchase Order Arrives!

When it arrives, rejoice! Verify that all the details are correct, then place the order with CreateSpace, being sure to list the ship-to destination as the school's shipping address as specified in the purchase order. Do not, in your excitement, use your default personal address. (If you do mess up, call CreateSpace or Ingram Customer Service immediately.)

Then draw up an invoice, spelling out the terms. (There are any number of templates on the Internet, such as ones at invoicehome.com, as well as those in Microsoft Word.) Use your publishing entity's information (not yours), the school, the purchase order number, the number of copies, the title, the shipping cost if you aren't providing it for free, and the total amount due. Feel free to list the terms as due in 30 days, even though it'll be ignored, and also "No Returns." I note the expected delivery date, as indicated by CreateSpace or Ingram. Attach a photocopy of the purchase order—not the original!—and mail it.

(For an example, see the Web Supplements page at pentucketpublishing.com.)

Email the principal, informing her that the copies have been ordered and let her know the expected delivery date. Thank her for her cooperation. Let her know—but only if this is something that interests you—that you'd be happy to speak to the students after they've read your book.

Then ask for one more thing that could be very important to you. Ask if someone at the school, either her as principal or the original recommending teacher or the ELA chair, would be willing to give a quote about your book and what they liked about it, since you're hoping other schools will adopt it as well. You don't have to push hard, but a simple request will often bear important fruit. If you get a good quote, that becomes front and center in your next set of promotional materials.

There's not much else left to do other than keep an eye on the books being delivered, especially if there's a moderately tight deadline. Typically, CreateSpace will email you when they are shipped, although there was one cardiac-arrest exception for me that required contacting Customer Service to be sure.

That, and wait for your invoice to be paid.

Oh yeah, one other thing.

Celebrate!

You may need to limit anything that involves spending money until that wonderful check arrives, and that cash flow noose gets removed from your neck, but celebrate!

Hug the people that mean the most to you. Hug yourself. You are special.

You aren't just special. You are awesome!

And you will be affecting all those kids in that school in a positive way.

You are making a difference.

CHAPTER 17

What's Next?

Write your next book! You've already written one that separated itself from all others. Do it again. And again.

You've got it in you. You've proven it.

Update the online description for the book that was selected to note that it has been adopted by high schools. Add that credit to your bio and to the "About the Author" section at the end of all your books.

Send a publicity release to your local newspaper. You're hot stuff! Let people know it! You might get a few new readers that way, and perhaps word of mouth will lead to even more successes.

Plan your next campaign, using the success of this one, especially any testimonials from the school.

More than anything, though, write your next book.

Acknowledgements

Thanks to the many fellow writers and friends who provided vital information for this book. Maggie Lynch and Darcy Pattison were phenomenal, investing hours of their time to provide me with important insights. They also acted as first readers, as did Tonya D. Price, Johanna Rothman, and Rigel Ailur. I'm indebted to you all.

Kim Mainord, Dean Wesley Smith, my brothers Steve and Ray, Mary Fishler-Fisk, Christina York, and Katharina Gerlach all contributed in areas of expertise where I sorely needed help.

To Dayle Dermatis, for the impressive editing skills she puts to work on all my books, and also for her prowess at book design to which I refer in these pages. Of course, any typos or errors that remain are entirely my own fault.

I might never have written any books if not for the influence and teaching of Kristine Kathryn Rusch and Dean Wesley Smith. And I *certainly* wouldn't have written a book about the business of writing. What amazing, life-changing mentors they have been.

And to all my other friends and family, for their love and support.

About the Author

David H. Hendrickson's first novel, *Cracking the Ice*, was praised by *Booklist* as "a gripping account of a courageous young man rising above evil." He has since published five additional novels, including *Offside*, which has been adopted for high school student required reading.

His short fiction has appeared in *Ellery Queen's Mystery Magazine* and numerous anthologies, including multiple issues of *Fiction River*.

Hendrickson has published well over one thousand works of nonfiction ranging from sports journalism to humor and essays. He has been honored with the Joe Concannon Hockey East Media Award and the Murray Kramer Scarlet Quill Award.

Get a free short story and be notified of new releases by signing up for his mailing list at www.hendricksonwriter.com.

A Special Request from the Author: Word of mouth is crucial for any author to succeed. If you enjoyed this book, please consider leaving a review where you purchased it. Even if it's only a line or two, it would make all the difference and would be very much appreciated.

Printed in Great Britain
by Amazon